99+CLEAN HACKS

MINIMALIST HABITS TO DECLUTTER YOUR HOME & RESET YOUR MIND

HUNG DO

99+
CLEAN
HACKS

MINIMALIST HABITS TO DECLUTTER
YOUR HOME & RESET YOUR MIND

*Feel lighter, think clearer, and
love your space again*

HUNG DO

ISBN:

Imprint: Independently published

https://bringhacks.com

For those who understand that progress isn't loud or flashy.

It's gentle, it's quiet, and it matters.

TABLE OF CONTENTS

Introduction - A Different Kind of Clean

Not so long ago, I lived by a quiet belief: that a clean home would promise me a clean life.

I polished surfaces until they shone. Lined up shoes in neat rows. Stacked towels with edges razor-sharp. I thought if everything looked perfect, I would finally feel perfect inside too - calm, steady, enough.

It never worked.

No matter how many corners I scrubbed, the deeper clutter remained - the kind you can't see but always feel. The kind that lives in the nervous system, not just the linen closet.

Because cleaning isn't about appearances. It's about energy. It's about creating spaces where your body can breathe easier, your mind can soften, and your spirit can exhale.

Your home isn't just four walls and a roof. It's a mirror of your inner world. When your environment feels forgiving, welcoming, lovingly tended - even in its imperfections - your whole being responds.

This book isn't about turning your home into a showroom. It's about turning it into a sanctuary.

It's not about punishing schedules or impossible standards. It's not about erasing every mess as proof of your worth.

It's about tiny, healing resets. It's about small, human motions - the kind that say, "I care for this space, and I care for the life unfolding inside it."

Inside these pages, you'll find 99+ simple, gentle "clean hacks." Not commands. Not obligations. Invitations. Each one is designed to lighten your space, soothe your mind, and help you reconnect with the ease that's already within you.

You don't have to become someone you're not. You don't have to finish everything at once. You don't have to make it look perfect to make it feel better.

You just have to begin. One square foot. One deep breath. One sock moved from here to there.

Healing isn't in the finished photo. It's in the movement. The tending. The loving.

If you're tired of chasing perfection and ready to build peace - small, steady, true - you're in the right place.

Ready?

Let's begin. One tiny reset at a time.

1.

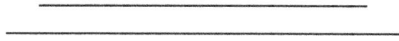

Reset to Breathe: Start from the Smallest Corners

PART 1 - Reset to Breathe: Start from the Smallest Corners

---

1. Your home is not a project - it's where your nervous system rests

For years, many of us have treated our homes like ongoing projects. There is always something to upgrade, fix, or organize. But here's the truth few talk about:

Your home isn't meant to impress others. It's meant to comfort you.

When you cross your threshold, your body should soften, not stiffen. Your breath should deepen, not constrict. Your heart should feel like it's returning home, not preparing for battle.

Neuroscience Insight:

Small environmental signals deeply affect the autonomic nervous system. A welcoming, non-judgmental home helps the body shift into "rest and digest" mode, calming anxiety and fostering healing.

Story:

Emma used to feel a pit in her stomach every time she entered her apartment, always scanning for what was unfinished. When she shifted her mindset to "this place holds me," even imperfect spaces started feeling like safety.

Try This Today:

When you step into your home, don't scan for flaws. Look for something that feels safe - a favorite chair, a framed photo, the scent of familiarity. Anchor yourself there. Let that small piece of home remind you: you are already held.

Mini Reset:
After you walk through your door and notice a safe object, close your eyes. Take three deep breaths. Feel your body soften.

Whisper to Yourself:
"I don't have to fix everything to deserve peace."

---

2. Don't clean everything - just rescue one square foot

Overwhelm freezes the mind. A messy room can feel like a tidal wave.

Instead of aiming to clean it all, zoom in. Rescue just one square foot. One corner of a nightstand. A single section of the counter.

Neuroscience Insight:
When the brain experiences overwhelm, its problem-solving center gets hijacked. Narrowing focus helps re-engage calm action pathways.

Story:

After a long illness, Mateo felt buried by clutter. He cleared just one corner of his nightstand - a lamp, a book, and a small clock. That tiny island of order became his launching point back to strength.

Try This Today:

Pick a tiny spot right now. Clear it completely. Feel the shift, however small. Let that little victory be enough for today.

Mini Reset:

After clearing your tiny space, smile at it. Acknowledge the shift you created.

Whisper to Yourself:

"Small victories are real victories."

---

3. Feel stuck? Just move one sock

When clutter paralyzes you, forget about decluttering. Forget about systems.

Just move one sock.

It seems ridiculous - but it's a doorway. One sock leads to two. Two to a basket. A basket to a cleaner floor.

Starting small isn't a weakness. It's wisdom.

Neuroscience Insight:

Movement activates the motor cortex, which stimulates motivation centers. Any movement - even tiny - can restart momentum.

Story:

Julia sat on the floor of her living room, overwhelmed. She spotted a single sock. With tears in her eyes, she moved it to the laundry basket. That sock became her first step back to agency.

Quick Tip:

When inertia grabs you, answer back with absurdly tiny actions.

Try This Today:

Move one object. Celebrate the shift from stillness to motion.

Mini Reset:

After moving the sock, place your hand over your heart and say, "I moved. I started."

Whisper to Yourself:

"One sock is not silly. It's sacred."

Mini-Section - Your Home as a Mirror

Your home doesn't just reflect your habits. It reflects your emotional state.

An overcrowded closet can mirror indecision.
A chaotic desk can mirror scattered thoughts.
A peaceful corner can mirror an oasis of hope.

When you change your space, even in tiny ways, you signal to your brain: "Transformation is possible."

This is why starting small matters. You are not just picking up objects. You are reclaiming trust in your own power to create peace.

Gentle Practice:

Today, find one small space that feels heavy. Lighten it, not to impress anyone, but to remind yourself: change begins with one breath, one step, one square foot.

Checklist: 5 Tiny Steps You Can Try Today:

- Clear your sink.
- Rescue one square foot.
- Move one sock.
- Protect one surface.
- Set an emotional intention at a doorway.

And if you wonder why these small actions feel surprisingly powerful, the answer lies deep within your brain's wiring.

Mini-Section - The Science of Micro-Reset

Tiny resets create powerful neurological shifts.

Every small action - moving a sock, wiping a sink, straightening a chair - activates the brain's reward circuitry. Dopamine is released, creating a sense of satisfaction and momentum.

Repeated small wins build what psychologists call "success spirals" - each success strengthens belief in your ability to change.

Micro-resets also calm the nervous system by engaging the parasympathetic "rest and digest" response. When your brain perceives order and small victories, it stops scanning for threats.

Gentle Thought:

Every sock moved, every sink cleared is not just tidying. It is retraining your mind to believe: "I am capable. I am safe. I can create change."

Try This Today:

After completing any tiny reset, whisper to yourself: "This small act matters."

---

4. The doorway trick - Reset your energy in 2 minutes

Before cleaning a room, pause at the doorway.

Ask yourself: "What energy do I want this space to hold?"

Is it calm? Creativity? Warmth?

Then step inside with purpose. Touch just one object that doesn't match the energy you seek - and remove it.

Neuroscience Insight:
Setting an intention primes your brain to notice opportunities that align with your goal. One touch, guided by purpose, can shift the entire atmosphere.

Story:
Whenever Kayla felt scattered, she paused at the threshold of her bedroom, closed her eyes, and whispered, "I choose calm." She removed one stray jacket off the bed. Her heart rate slowed instantly.

Try This Today:
Today, stand in a doorway. Set an emotional

intention before you clean. Watch how the space responds.

Mini Reset:
After removing one object, breathe in deeply, imagining the new energy you are inviting in.

Whisper to Yourself:
"I am shaping this space, and it is shaping me."

---

5. Your sink is a reset button - here's why it matters

When life feels too heavy, don't try to fix everything.

Just clear the sink.

A sparkling sink is a symbol. It tells your mind, "I can create order. I am capable."

Neuroscience Insight:
Completing small physical tasks boosts serotonin, enhancing feelings of competence and calm.

Story:

After losing her job, Alina couldn't organize her house. She focused only on keeping her kitchen sink clear. That small oasis of order became the first brick in rebuilding her life.

Try This Today:

If today spirals out of control, rescue the sink. Rinse. Wipe. Shine. Reclaim a piece of peace.

Mini Reset:

After shining the sink, pause and let your shoulders relax. Let the small sparkle echo inside you.

Whisper to Yourself:

"This small clean space means I am not lost."

---

6. Leave one clear space and protect it like it's sacred

You don't need a perfect home to feel anchored. You need one protected space.

Choose a corner - a desk, a nightstand, a chair.

Clear it completely. Guard it fiercely.

This tiny oasis becomes a visual lifeline. Every glance at it reminds your nervous system: "There is calm here."

Neuroscience Insight:
Consistent visual cues of order help regulate the vagus nerve, enhancing feelings of emotional safety.

Story:
When grieving, Alex cleared just the surface of his nightstand. Every morning, seeing that small uncluttered space helped him breathe deeper.

Try This Today:
Pick one surface. Clear it today. Defend it tenderly, like you would defend a flame from the wind.

Mini Reset:
After clearing your sacred space, sit nearby for one full minute. Let its calmness soak into your bones.

Whisper to Yourself:

"This space is my lighthouse."

---

7. Don't chase a clean house - create a calmer you

A spotless home is a moving target. Life brings mess, and always will.

If peace depends on perfection, you'll always feel like you're losing.

Shift the goal:

Create a calmer you.

Every tiny act of tidying isn't about achieving visual perfection. It's about carving out moments of mental relief.

Neuroscience Insight:

Focusing on internal states (how you feel) rather than external appearances nurtures long-term resilience.

Story:

Elena stopped judging her house by Instagram standards. She began asking, "Does this room help me breathe easier?" Her home transformed without the burden of perfectionism.

Try This Today:

The next time you clean, don't ask, "How can I make this flawless?" Ask, "How can I make this feel lighter?"

Mini Reset:

As you clean today, periodically ask: "Is this making me feel lighter?" Adjust gently if needed.

Whisper to Yourself:

"My calm matters more than appearances."

2.

———————
———————

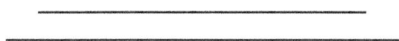

Lighten the Load: Small Habits, Big Relief

PART 2 - Lighten the Load:
Small Habits, Big Relief

---

1. Do it when you're already standing - the "one motion" rule

Momentum is precious. Once you're moving, keep moving.

After brushing your teeth, wipe the sink. After putting on your shoes, straighten the mat. After grabbing your jacket, adjust the coats nearby.

Story: Anna realized that every time she paused between small tasks, the mess piled up. By linking a tiny cleanup to an action she was already doing, her home stayed lighter without extra effort.

Neuroscience Insight: Linking a new habit to an existing movement pattern uses the brain's "synaptic tagging" process, making it easier for behaviors to stick without exhausting willpower.

Layer of Meaning: Every seamless action you create becomes a silent affirmation that you are capable of gentle progress.

Try This Today: After your next small action, tack on one micro-cleanup. Let flow carry you, not force.

Mini Reset: After completing the motion, smile softly to yourself. Let movement feel like music.

Whisper to Yourself: "Momentum is my ally."

2. Make the mess visible - so your future self won't ignore it

Hidden messes grow silently. Visibility creates gentle accountability.

Instead of hiding clutter behind closet doors or stuffing it into drawers, place it kindly in sight. Not to shame yourself - but to remind yourself.

Story: Whenever Mia hid unsorted mail in a drawer, it lingered for weeks. When she placed it in a clear tray by the front door, she felt compelled to sort it every few days. Visibility made change easier, not heavier.

Practical Insight: Out-of-sight clutter still weighs on the subconscious mind. Visibility brings it into conscious care.

Layer of Meaning: Choosing to see your mess with compassion instead of judgment is itself a revolution.

Try This Today: Choose one hidden pile. Bring it out where you can see it gently. Let kindness - not guilt - guide you.

Mini Reset: As you look at a visible mess, take one calming breath. It is not shameful. It is an invitation.

Whisper to Yourself: "Seeing is the first step to healing."

---

3. Create a "guilt-free" decluttering box

Letting go can feel complicated. Permission eases the path.

Designate a "Maybe Later - No Pressure" box. Place inside anything you are unsure about keeping. No forced decisions. Only space and grace.

Story: After her father's passing, Nora struggled to let go of worn-out books she didn't truly love.

Creating a guilt-free box allowed her to honor memories without being imprisoned by them.

Gentle Reminder: Not every decision needs to be made today. Time reveals what the heart already knows.

Layer of Meaning: Honoring hesitation is honoring your humanity.

Try This Today: Start your "guilt-free" box. Let future clarity be your guide.

Mini Reset: As you place an item inside, breathe out guilt. Breathe in peace.

Whisper to Yourself: "Release does not erase love."

---

4. The 2-minute rule that actually works

If something takes less than 2 minutes, do it now.

Wipe the table. Sort the envelope. Hang the towel.

Story: Leo realized he spent more energy avoiding tiny tasks than actually doing them. Embracing the 2-minute rule freed his mind from the endless weight of "later."

Neuroscience Insight: Quick wins trigger micro-rewards in the brain, building confidence and creating a success momentum loop.

Layer of Meaning: Each tiny completed task is a promise kept to your future self.

Try This Today: Complete one lingering task that will take less than 2 minutes. Watch how your spirit lifts.

Mini Reset: After completing a micro-task, pause. Let the satisfaction ripple outward.

Whisper to Yourself: "Small actions hold big magic."

Mini-Section - Emotional Reward Loops: Why Tiny Wins Matter

Tiny victories do more than tidy your space. They rewire your emotional landscape.

When you finish a small task, your brain releases dopamine, the chemical of reward and motivation. But something deeper happens too: your mind whispers, "I can trust myself."

Each completed tiny habit builds not just competence, but self-respect.

Gentle Practice: After each small win, pause. Notice the warmth blooming inside. It is not about perfection - it is about returning to self-trust, one breath at a time.

Gentle Thought: Every small win is a stitch in the fabric of your resilience.

---

5. Clean less, more often - the surprising secret of tidy people

Consistency beats intensity.

Tidy homes are not built by occasional deep cleans, but by small, frequent resets.

Story: Sofia set a 7-minute evening timer to reset her kitchen counters. Over months, the habit turned into an effortless rhythm of care - never overwhelming, always sustainable.

Practical Insight: Habits thrive when they are light enough to carry even on heavy days.

Layer of Meaning: Gentle repetition carves peace deeper into the day.

Try This Today: Set a 5-10 minute timer tonight. Tidy gently, stop when it rings. Trust accumulation over ambition.

Mini Reset: After the timer ends, thank yourself. You showed up.

Whisper to Yourself: "Consistency is my quiet revolution."

---

6. No motivation? Clean like you're procrastinating

Motivation is unreliable. Movement is not.

Use cleaning as a way to gently dodge bigger tasks without self-judgment. Productive procrastination still moves life forward.

Story: Facing a stressful project, Eli would organize his bookshelf. The small victory grounded him, making the harder task seem more approachable afterward.

Gentle Reflection: All motion matters. Playfulness turns avoidance into quiet progress.

Layer of Meaning: Even sidesteps can be sacred when they lead toward lightness.

Try This Today: If you're stuck avoiding something, clean one tiny thing. Let procrastination carry you kindly.

Mini Reset: As you clean, notice: movement opens hidden doors.

Whisper to Yourself: "Every step forward counts."

Mini-Section - The Hidden Strength of Gentle Habits

Gentle habits are strong because they don't require fighting yourself. They grow like vines - quietly, steadily, wrapping life in grace.

Each tiny reset is a seed. Each breath of effortless maintenance is sunlight.

The secret is not harsh discipline. It is patient kindness.

Gentle Practice: This week, instead of setting harsh goals, set soft promises:

- I will move with kindness.
- I will begin small.
- I will trust that little by little is enough.

Gentle Thought: Gentle habits do not shout. But they rebuild whole worlds.

Checklist: Gentle Systems to Try This Week

- Link one tiny cleanup to an existing habit.
- Bring one hidden mess into kind visibility.
- Create a guilt-free decluttering box.
- Complete one 2-minute task immediately.
- Set a 5-10 minute evening reset timer. Turn avoidance into motion with a playful task.

Remember: Tiny shifts ripple wider than you imagine.

3.

Mind Meets Mess: Healing Through Cleaning

PART 3 - Mind Meets Mess: Healing Through Cleaning

---

1. Decluttering anxiety is real - and it's not your fault

If you've ever stared at a messy room and felt paralyzed, you're not broken. You're human.

Clutter triggers stress because every unfinished pile whispers, "You're behind. You're failing."

Story: After months of struggling with depression, Lena found herself frozen in her living room, surrounded by laundry and papers. She wasn't lazy. She was overwhelmed by invisible emotional weights attached to each object.

Neuroscience Insight: Visual clutter increases cortisol levels, leading to heightened stress responses. Your brain interprets unfinished tasks as open loops demanding attention, draining emotional energy.

Layer of Meaning: Feeling overwhelmed by a mess is not a flaw. It is your sensitive system responding naturally to visual overload.

Try This Today: Choose one single item within reach. Decide its fate. One choice quiets a thousand noisy doubts.

Mini Reset: After choosing, place your hand over your heart and whisper, "I moved forward."

Whisper to Yourself: "Overwhelm is not my identity."

---

2. Clean to the rhythm of your emotions - not against them

Some days you are energized. Other days, grief or weariness pulls at your feet.

Honor that.

Match your cleaning to your emotional weather.

Story: After a hard week, Sara could not muster the energy to clean her kitchen. Instead, she slowly wiped down just the coffee table while soft music played. It was enough. It mattered.

Gentle Reflection: You are not a machine. Your actions can be a duet with your emotions, not a fight against them.

Layer of Meaning: Moving with your feelings creates cooperation inside you instead of more conflict.

Try This Today: Notice your energy level today. Choose a task that matches it. Tiny or grand - both are worthy.

Mini Reset: After completing the task, take one deep breath of permission.

Whisper to Yourself: "I flow with myself, not against."

---

3. Anger, grief, boredom - turn them into movement

Emotions are energy. If bottled up, they fester. If channeled, they heal.

Scrub counters when anger simmers. Fold laundry while grieving. Sort a drawer during restless boredom.

Story: After a painful breakup, Nathan couldn't sit still. Instead of stewing, he cleaned out an entire closet, crying and breathing as he worked. The clearing of space became a clearing of sorrow.

Neuroscience Insight: Physical movement during emotional arousal helps regulate the limbic system, allowing intense feelings to process and release.

Layer of Meaning: Motion is a language that emotions understand.

Try This Today: Notice what you feel. Let it move you toward one small physical task.

Mini Reset: As you move, repeat silently: "I am shifting energy."

Whisper to Yourself: "Movement is medicine."

---

4. When you can't clean, sit in a clean space instead

Some days, even lifting a hand feels impossible.

That is okay.

Healing sometimes looks like sitting gently inside the calm that already exists.

Story: During deep burnout, Leo couldn't clean his entire apartment. But he kept one chair clear. Every evening, he sat in that chair, breathing. It became his anchor back to life.

Gentle Reminder: Stillness can be an act of power, not surrender.

Layer of Meaning: You deserve peace even on days you cannot create it.

Try This Today: Find one clean surface. Sit nearby. Let it hold you without expectation.

Mini Reset: As you rest, whisper to the space, "Thank you for keeping me."

Whisper to Yourself: "Even resting, I am healing."

---

5. The story behind the clutter matters more than the stuff

Objects are not just things. They are emotional echoes.

A ticket stub, a worn-out sweater, a broken trinket - each carries layers of meaning.

Story: Sofia kept a cracked mug from college because it reminded her of lost friendships. When she finally released it, she wasn't discarding the memory - she was making space for new ones.

Gentle Reflection: Decluttering is not about ruthlessness. It is about making conscious choices about what stories to carry forward.

Layer of Meaning: Letting go is not erasing the past. It is choosing your future.

Try This Today: Hold one difficult object. Ask: "Does this help me move forward?" Honor the answer.

Mini Reset: As you release an item, thank it silently for its place in your story.

Whisper to Yourself: "I choose what I carry."

Mini-Section - Cleaning Through Emotions

Cleaning is often portrayed as mechanical. But for those seeking healing, it becomes emotional alchemy.

Each wipe of a counter, each folded shirt, each item placed with care is a ritual of self-acknowledgment:

- I am still here.
- I still matter.
- I can still shape my world, even in small ways.

When you move through a mess with tenderness, you move through your own emotional debris, too.

Gentle Practice: Next time you clean, whisper silently: "This is how I reclaim my place in the world."

Gentle Thought: Your healing is stitched into every gentle motion you make.

Mini-Section - Mess as Fertile Ground

There is fertile ground beneath every scattered paper, every forgotten pile, every dusty corner.

Mess is not a verdict. It is potential.

Just as a forest floor must gather fallen leaves to nurture the next season of life, your cluttered spaces hold the raw material for your renewal.

Mess means you have lived. You have tried. You have gathered dreams, memories, and mistakes.

Gentle Thought: Your task is not to erase the mess with shame. Your task is to sift through it with tenderness and plant new seeds inside the clearing you create.

Each object released is mulch for new growth. Each square foot cleared is soil turned toward the sun.

Gentle Practice: Next time you clear a space, whisper to yourself: "I am not undoing my life. I am making room for it to bloom."

Mini-Section - Mess is Memory, Too

Clutter is not just stuff. It is memory-stacked, scattered, and stored.

Every book on the shelf, every note tucked away, every worn-out item carries whispers of moments you once lived.

When you sort through a mess, you are not just tidying objects. You are curating your story.

Gentle Thought: Your past does not need to be erased to make space for your future. It needs to be honored, sifted, and carried forward with care.

As you can see, let yourself smile at the memories you cherish. Let yourself thank and release the ones you no longer need to carry.

Gentle Practice: Today, when you pick up an old object, pause. Whisper: "I honor the life this held. I now make space for the life I am building."

Mini-Section - Cleaning with Gratitude

Let letting go become an act of thanksgiving.

Before you release an item - a tattered sweater, a chipped mug, a paper from a life chapter closed - pause.

Place your hand on it. Thank it silently:

- "Thank you for carrying me."
- "Thank you for witnessing a part of my journey."
- "Thank you for being here when I needed you."
  Then, release it with love, not regret.

Gentle Thought: Gratitude transforms goodbye into a blessing.

Gentle Practice: This week, as you declutter, let every farewell be wrapped in gratitude.

Mini-Section - Cleaning as Meditation

You do not need to sit cross-legged to meditate.

You can meditate while wiping a table. While folding a towel. While moving one sock.

Cleaning Meditation Mini-Exercise:

- Choose a tiny task: wiping, folding, straightening.
- As your hands move, breathe slowly. With each movement, silently affirm:
    + "I clear space outside."
    + "I clear space inside."
    + "I create peace with each touch."

Let your motions be prayers stitched into the fabric of ordinary life.

Gentle Thought: Every hand that moves with kindness turns cleaning into sacredness.

Checklist: Emotional Cleaning Rituals

Tiny Action - Inner Intention:

- Move one sock - "I shift my energy."
- Wipe a table - "I create peace."
- Sit in a clear chair - "I allow stillness to heal me."
- Fold a blanket - "I wrap myself in care."
- Sort one drawer - "I organize not just objects, but my thoughts."

Remember: Tiny movements create spacious hearts.

4.

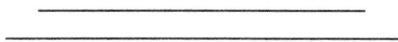

Flow & Function: Design Your Space to Support You

PART 4 - Flow & Function: Design Your Space to Support You

1. Stop organizing what you should be letting go of

Organizing is not always the answer. Sometimes, it's a beautiful delay tactic.

Story: Emma owned dozens of labeled bins for clothes she never wore. She spent weekends arranging and rearranging them, convincing herself she was "making progress." True peace only came when she asked the harder question: "What if I simply don't need this?"

Gentle Insight:

You cannot organize excess into serenity. Release first. Arrange second.

Layer of Meaning:

True freedom often requires subtraction, not smarter storage.

Try This Today:

Choose one "organized" pile today. Ask yourself honestly: "Would I choose this if I were starting fresh?" If not, thank it - and let it go.

Mini Reset:

After releasing even one item, breathe deeply into the space it leaves behind.

Whisper to Yourself:

"I clear not to perfect, but to breathe."

2. Function first - it doesn't have to look like Pinterest

A beautiful home is a functional home - not just a photogenic one.

Story: Tom rearranged his living room three times, trying to mimic magazine layouts. It wasn't until he prioritized flow for his family's game nights that the room finally felt like home.

Gentle Reflection:

Beauty follows use. Not the other way around.

Layer of Meaning:

A home that serves you will always outshine a home that performs for others.

Try This Today:

Walk through one room today. Ask, "Does this layout serve the way I live and love?" Move one thing to make it easier.

Mini Reset:

Celebrate functionality over facade.

Whisper to Yourself:

"My home is for living, not displaying."

---

3. Create "drop zones" where mess is allowed

Mess will happen. Life guarantees it. The secret is in containing it kindly.

Story: Without a landing spot, Leo lost his keys almost daily. A simple bowl by the door changed his mornings - and his stress levels.

Practical Insight:

Inviting clutter into designated spaces keeps chaos from colonizing everywhere.

Layer of Meaning:

Compassionate systems reduce daily self-blame.

Try This Today:

Identify one clutter magnet (keys, mail, bags). Create a forgiving "drop zone."

Mini Reset:

Smile when you toss something into your new zone. It's working.

Whisper to Yourself:

"Systems serve my humanness."

---

4. One in, one out - the timeless declutter rule

Sustainability is simpler than we imagine.

Story: Olivia decided: every time she bought a book, she would donate one. Her shelves stayed intentional, and her reading felt lighter.

Gentle Reflection:

Joy shouldn't smother itself with accumulation.

Layer of Meaning:

Growth is expansion paired with discernment.

Try This Today:

Apply "one in, one out" to one area of your life

this week - shoes, mugs, notebooks. Feel the space open.

Mini Reset:

Each exit is an entryway for clarity.

Whisper to Yourself:

"Enough is a beautiful word."

---

5. Make clean-up easier than the mess

People follow the path of least resistance. Spaces should, too.

Story: Mia noticed her family never used the fancy shoe rack that required opening two doors. Switching to a simple open basket cut the hallway mess by 80%.

Practical Insight:

Lower the effort required to stay tidy. Raise the effort required to make a mess.

Layer of Meaning:

Make doing the right thing the easy thing.

Try This Today:

Identify one "friction point" at home. Simplify it shamelessly.

Mini Reset:

After making tidiness effortless, breathe in the relief.

Whisper to Yourself:

"Ease is a form of wisdom."

Mini-Section - Designing for Real Life

You don't live inside a catalog. You live inside a heartbeat.

Design is not about creating a showroom. It's about crafting a stage where your daily life can unfold with less friction and more grace.

- If your kids dump backpacks by the door, add a basket there.
- If your coffee table is always cluttered, clear it and leave only a candle and a book you love.
- If your bathroom counter invites chaos, offer it small containers to corral the storm.

Gentle Thought:

Design for how you live, not how you wish you lived.

Gentle Practice:

Today, adjust one tiny corner to fit your real habits. Real life deserves real support.

Mini-Section - Space That Supports

Your environment either pulls you forward or holds you back.

A supportive space whispers:

- "It's easy to begin."
- "You are welcome to rest."
- "Your effort flows here, not fights here."

Gentle Reflection:

You deserve spaces that cheer for your thriving.

Try This Today:

Choose one surface today. Simplify it until it feels like an open invitation rather than an obligation.

Whisper to Yourself:

"I deserve spaces that are on my side."

Mini-Section - Friction Points and Flow Boosters

Every home has friction points - those little obstacles that create resistance:

- Shoes pile up at the entrance.
- Mail scatters across the table.
- Dishes linger by the sink.

Instead of fighting your habits, design to support them.

Flow Boosters:

- A large tray for the daily mail.
- An open basket for quick shoe drops.
- Hooks instead of hangers for jackets.

Gentle Reflection:

When you reduce friction for the behaviors you want, ease becomes your ally.

Gentle Practice:

Today, identify one small friction point. Create a flow booster for it.

Whisper to Yourself:

"I design with kindness, not judgment."

Mini-Section - Case Study: A Room Reset

Before:

Maria's bedroom overwhelmed her. Clothes on

every chair, a nightstand buried in clutter, a desk she avoided.

She dreamed of a sanctuary but felt paralyzed.

Tiny Steps:

- She added a basket at the door for worn clothes.
- Cleared her nightstand, leaving only a lamp and a favorite book.
Moved her desk near the window for better light and placed a plant beside it.

After:

Maria's bedroom became a retreat - not by buying new furniture, but by removing friction and honoring how she truly lived.

Gentle Thought:

You don't need a new home. You need a new relationship with your space.

Gentle Practice:

Choose one room. Imagine how it could feel more supportive. Take one tiny step today.

Checklist: Gentle Home Flow Upgrades

Simple Changes to Boost Ease:

- Place an open basket for shoes at the entrance.
- Add a tray for mail near the door.
- Keep only one or two items on countertops.
- Use hooks instead of hangers for daily jackets.
- Store daily items (keys, wallet) in a visible, dedicated spot.
- Simplify bedside tables to essentials only.
- Place a donation box somewhere accessible.
- Use open shelving where closed doors add resistance.

Gentle Reminder:

Design for the life you live, not the life you "should" have.

Mini-Section - The Energy of Flowing Spaces

Spaces that flow are not just easier to maintain - they make living itself lighter.

When you walk into a room where movement feels effortless, your body responds. Shoulders drop. Breath deepens. Energy lifts.

Gentle Reflection:
Flowing spaces aren't about perfection. They are about relief. They are about creating places where being alive feels a little easier.

Gentle Practice:
Stand in the middle of a room today. Notice how your body feels. If tension rises, find one small adjustment to make movement freer.

Whisper to Yourself:
"Ease is nourishment."

Mini-Section - Space Rituals: Tiny Habits for Big Shifts

Daily rituals are the secret language of supportive homes.

Simple Space Rituals:

- Open a window for 5 minutes each morning.
- Clear one surface before bed.
- Touch a favorite object each day and say "thank you."
- Light a candle when you reset a room.

Gentle Thought:

Tiny rituals weave steadiness into the fabric of our days.

Gentle Practice:

Choose one ritual today. Let it anchor you back to ease.

Checklist: Daily Flow Rituals

Morning:

- Open a window to refresh the air.
- Make your bed with presence.

Midday:

- Clear one surface.
- Drink water mindfully.

Evening:

- Reset one small area (desk, nightstand, couch).
- Dim the lights and soften your space.

Gentle Reminder:

Small daily acts create spacious living.

5.

Sustain the Peace: Gentle Systems for Real Life

PART 5 - Sustain the Peace: Gentle Systems for Real Life

---

1. Habits that survive bad days - not just good intentions

Good intentions are easy on good days. True systems survive the hard ones.

Story: When Lucas felt energized, he vacuumed the whole house. When he felt low, he still managed to reset the living room because he had built a habit small enough to survive exhaustion.

Gentle Insight: Design systems that feel doable even on your worst days. That's how real change lasts.

Layer of Meaning: Resilience isn't about force. It's about designing with compassion.

Try This Today: Choose one micro-habit you can complete even when you're tired. Commit to it for one week.

Mini Reset: After completing it, smile gently. Proof of grace.

Whisper to Yourself: "Consistency is kindness to my future self."

---

2. Tiny resets throughout the day that change everything

Tiny resets create invisible scaffolding for your peace.

Straighten a chair. Fold a blanket. Wipe a counter. Each act anchors you back to presence.

Story: Sara found that adjusting one small thing each hour kept her space (and mind) from spiraling into overwhelm by day's end.

Practical Insight: Small resets prevent big chaos.

Layer of Meaning: Tiny acts are quiet declarations: I care for this life.

Try This Today: Set a gentle alarm every 2-3 hours today. When it chimes, reset one small thing nearby.

Mini Reset: Feel the shift ripple outward.

Whisper to Yourself: "Small steadies my soul."

---

3. Cleaning loops - and how to gently break them

Ever feel stuck in cycles?

- Tidy up.
- Life happens.
- Everything explodes.
- Start over, exhausted.

Breaking the loop starts with recognizing it without judgment.

Story: Ella realized her clutter always started with laundry. By building a better laundry system (smaller loads, more often), she disrupted the whole messy cycle.

Gentle Reflection: Find the first domino. Focus there.

Layer of Meaning: Heal the pattern, not just the symptom.

Try This Today: Trace today's mess back to its first small cause. Imagine one gentle adjustment.

Mini Reset: Smile at the first small change. It matters.

Whisper to Yourself: "One shift reshapes everything."

---

4. Reclaim your weekends - weekday systems that work

Weekends are meant for living, not catching up.

Small systems throughout the week protect your weekends from being swallowed by chores.

Story: Before changing her routine, Ana spent every Saturday cleaning. Now, by setting 15-minute resets each weekday evening, her Saturdays are free for picnics and bookstores.

Practical Insight: Spread small tasks wide, instead of stacking them high.

Layer of Meaning: Daily rhythms protect freedom.

Try This Today: Choose one small task to shift into your weekday rhythm this week.

Mini Reset: Feel Saturday breathe easier.

Whisper to Yourself: "I deserve spacious weekends."

---

5. Let go of "should" - build a rhythm that fits you

Not every rhythm works for every life.

Some thrive with nightly resets. Others need a big Sunday reset. Some clean best in the mornings. Others at midnight.

Story: Mateo felt guilty for not following a famous "cleaning checklist." When he finally built his own quirky, flexible rhythm, his home and heart both lightened.

Gentle Reflection: Freedom starts where "should" ends.

Layer of Meaning: Your peace deserves personalization.

Try This Today: Craft a rhythm that fits your real energy, real time, real life - not an imagined ideal.

Mini Reset: Celebrate the rhythm that feels like breathing.

Whisper to Yourself: "My way is worthy."

Mini-Section - Gentle Systems Grow Strong Roots

Gentle systems endure because they are made of kindness, not punishment.

When habits feel like acts of care, they anchor us.

They become invisible supports - scaffolding that holds our lives together even when storms come.

Gentle Thought: Consistency doesn't require perfection. It requires tenderness.

Gentle Practice: This week, notice one gentle habit you already have. Thank it.

Mini-Section - The Art of Sustainable Ease

Ease is an art form.

Building a life where peace is not something you chase, but something you live inside, requires intention.

Key Reminders:

- Lower friction for what nurtures you.
- Remove shame from imperfect days.
- Return to gentle rhythms again and again.

Gentle Thought: Ease is not laziness. Ease is design born from wisdom.

Gentle Practice: Simplify one process today - one drawer, one morning routine, one mental checklist.

Whisper to Yourself: "Ease is strength dressed in softness."

Mini-Section - Gentle Self-Repair Days

No system is perfect. Life will happen. Habits will break.

When your gentle systems stumble, respond with kindness, not criticism.

Designate "Self-Repair Days" - quiet pauses to breathe, assess, and reset lightly.

Self-Repair Steps:

- Rescue one tiny spot.
- Reset one drop zone.
- Breathe deeply and rest.

Gentle Thought: Falling behind doesn't erase all progress. Restarting is a strength.

Gentle Practice: Mark one day a month as your Self-Repair Day. Let it be a celebration of resilience.

Whisper to Yourself: "I honor my restarts."

Mini-Section - Seasonal Reset Rituals

Life flows in seasons. So should your spaces.

Seasonal Reset Ideas:

- **Spring:** Lighten your bedroom - swap heavy blankets for fresh sheets.
- **Summer:** Create an outdoor space to savor longer evenings.
- **Autumn:** Simplify your wardrobe for cooler days.
- **Winter:** Add soft lighting and cozy textures.

Gentle Reflection: Refreshing spaces with the seasons refreshes your spirit, too.

Gentle Practice: This week, welcome the current season with one tiny shift in your home.

Whisper to Yourself: "I flow with the seasons."

Bonus Checklist - Gentle System Recovery Plan

When You Feel Overwhelmed:

- Rescue one tiny square foot.
- Clear one drop zone.
- Make one surface breathable.
- Breathe. Rest.
- Begin again tomorrow.

Gentle Reminder: Resetting is not failing. It's choosing yourself again.

Checklist: Sustainable Gentle Systems

Daily Systems:

- Morning: Open blinds to let light in.
- Midday: Reset one surface.
- Evening: Return items to drop zones.

Weekly Systems:

- Monday: 10-minute laundry catch-up.
- Wednesday: 10-minute "invisible clutter" sweep (corners, counters).
- Friday: Refresh entryway or bedroom.

Monthly Systems:

- First weekend: Donate one bag.
- Mid-month: Reassess one drop zone or friction point.

Gentle Reminder: Small, rhythmic care builds lives that feel breathable.

Mini-Section - You Are the Keeper of the Flow

Your home is not a static object. It is a living, breathing extension of you.

Every time you straighten a pillow, wipe a table, rescue a corner - you are tending the flow of your life.

You are not just keeping a house. You are keeping a sanctuary.

Gentle Reflection: You are allowed to build a world that holds you softly.

Gentle Practice: Today, tend to one tiny space with full presence, knowing it reflects your care for yourself.

Whisper to Yourself: "I am the keeper of my peace."

Closing Reflection - Begin Again, Gently

There will be messy days. Busy seasons. Forgotten habits.

And there will always be another morning, another moment, another breath inviting you back to gentleness.

You are never starting from scratch. You are always starting from wisdom earned.

Gentle Thought: Progress is not a straight line. It is a spiral upward.

Final Whisper to Yourself: "I begin again. Gently. Always."

BONUS PART 1 - Declutter Your Digital Life

1. Digital Clutter is Real - and It Drains You

Just because you can't see it doesn't mean it isn't weighing you down.

Thousands of unread emails. Desktop icons crammed together. Notification pings piling up.

Story: After months of digital buildup, Mia realized she felt a strange anxiety every time she opened her laptop. Clearing her inbox and desktop brought an immediate, surprising sense of lightness.

Gentle Insight: Your digital spaces whisper to your nervous system, too.

Layer of Meaning: Clearing pixels clears mental static.

Try This Today: Delete 5 unused apps from your phone. Breathe into the space they leave behind.

Mini Reset: Feel your mind un-knot itself, even slightly.

Whisper to Yourself: "I deserve spaciousness in all dimensions."

---

2. Inbox Zero? Not Necessary - Inbox Calm? Yes.

Chasing perfection (zero emails) can become another stressor.

Instead, aim for **Inbox Calm**:

- Unsubscribe from newsletters you don't read.
- Create simple folders: "To Respond," "To Save," "To Delete."
- Batch-check emails instead of constant checking.

Story: Noah stopped checking emails every 10 minutes. Instead, he checked twice a day. His mind stopped buzzing like a mosquito swarm.

Gentle Reflection: Boundaries are a kindness to your brain.

Layer of Meaning: Silence can be something you create, not wait for.

Try This Today: Unsubscribe from 3 email lists you no longer need.

Mini Reset: Every email you release makes room for breath.

Whisper to Yourself: "I curate what enters my mind."

---

3. Photo Clutter - Captured Moments, Captured Energy

Thousands of unsorted photos create invisible mental drag.

Story: Elena spent a weekend deleting blurry, duplicate, and meaningless photos. What remained? Only joy.

Gentle Insight: Memories deserve sacred space, not digital noise.

Layer of Meaning: Choosing what to keep is choosing what to honor.

Try This Today: Delete 50 photos today. Trust your heart's memory more than your phone's memory.

Mini Reset: Keep photos that make you breathe deeper.

Whisper to Yourself: "I carry moments, not clutter."

---

4. Create Digital Drop Zones

Digital clutter needs homes, too.

Create a "Downloads to Sort" folder. Have a "Screenshots to Review" folder. Move saved links to a reading list, not random tabs.

Story: Jasper used to have 70 tabs open. Now, with a "To Read Later" folder, he browses lighter and lives clearer.

Practical Insight: Containment calms chaos.

Layer of Meaning: Systems are not burdens. They are bridges.

Try This Today: Create one new digital folder to hold temporary clutter.

Mini Reset: Smile at one tiny point of digital order.

Whisper to Yourself: "Even bits and bytes deserve homes."

Mini-Section - Digital Spaces Mirror Inner Spaces

Your devices are not separate from your emotional world.

A cluttered desktop often mirrors a cluttered mind. An overwhelmed inbox often mirrors an overwhelmed spirit.

Gentle Reflection: You are allowed to create spaces - both visible and invisible - that support your peace.

Gentle Practice: Today, clear one small digital corner. Feel how even one tiny clearing shifts the way your mind breathes.

Whisper to Yourself: "Clearing space outside clears space inside."

Deep Story - The Day I Deleted 5000 Photos

There was a Saturday when I faced the chaos - 5000 photos filling my phone.

Blurry meals, screenshots I no longer needed, photos I didn't even remember taking.

I sat with a warm cup of tea, deleting a few at a time. It was strange - deleting didn't feel like erasing. It felt like reclaiming.

By sunset, I kept only the images that made my heart stir. A flower I noticed after a hard day. A laugh frozen in time. A sunrise over a mountain I almost didn't climb.

I realized: I wasn't making space for emptiness. I was making space for meaning.

Gentle Thought: Not every memory is a home you need to carry.

Gentle Practice: Spend one hour this week curating your memories, not hoarding them.

Whisper to Yourself: "I carry only what sings inside me."

---

5. Reclaim Your Screen Time

You are allowed to take your time back from the endless scroll.

Tiny Practices:

- Turn off non-essential notifications.
- Create a "Tech-Free Hour" each evening.
- Move distracting apps off your home screen.

Story: After moving social media apps to a hidden folder, Dylan found himself reaching for a book more often than a screen.

Gentle Insight: Technology is a tool. Not a tether.

Layer of Meaning: Attention is sacred. Spend it like treasure.

Try This Today: Designate one "no-scroll" hour today. Notice what your mind does with the silence.

Mini Reset: Let your mind stretch in the new spaciousness.

Whisper to Yourself: "I am more than what I consume."

Bonus Checklist - Digital Boundaries for Gentle Living

Daily Practices:

- Close apps after using them.
- Unsubscribe from one email per day.
- Delete 10 photos.

Weekly Practices:

- Empty your Downloads folder.
- Sort new screenshots or delete them.
- Review screen time and adjust if needed.

Monthly Practices:

- Clean your desktop.
- Curate your saved articles or links.
- Reflect: What digital spaces nourish me? What drains me?

Gentle Reminder: Boundaries are not walls. They are gardens.

Mini-Section - Your Mind Is Your True Desktop

Your real workspace isn't your desk. It's your mind.

Every deleted file, every unsubscribed email, every sorted folder is an act of protection for your precious cognitive energy.

Gentle Thought: You are not a machine to process endless data. You are a being meant to savor life.

Gentle Practice: Tonight, close all open tabs before sleeping. Let your mind rest closed, too.

Whisper to Yourself: "I am allowed to shut down gracefully."

BONUS PART 2 - Tiny Mental Resets for Clarity

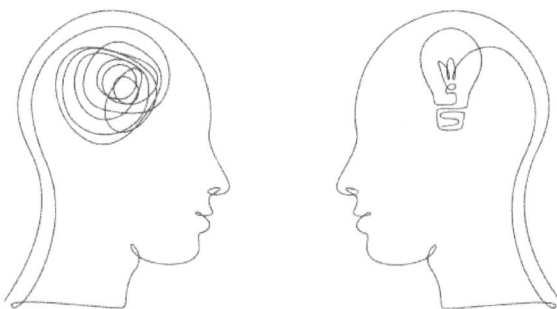

---

1. The Power of One Deep Breath

One breath. In. Out. Done with full presence.

Story: Amelia used to reach for her phone the moment she felt overwhelmed. Now, she pauses, places a hand over her heart, and takes one intentional breath. Most days, that breath is enough to interrupt the spiral.

Gentle Insight: You always carry a reset button inside your chest.

Layer of Meaning: Peace is just one breath deeper than panic.

Try This Today: Right now, close your eyes and take one slow, savoring breath.

Mini Reset: Notice how your shoulders soften even a little.

Whisper to Yourself: "I am allowed to slow down."

---

2. The 60-Second Sight Reset

Sometimes your mind isn't tired. Your eyes are.

Story: Julian felt drained at work without realizing he hadn't looked away from his laptop for hours. Now, every hour, he gazes out a window for 60 seconds. His headaches faded. His creativity returned.

Gentle Reflection: Your mind needs distance to dream.

Layer of Meaning: Perspective isn't just mental. It's physical too.

Try This Today: Every 90 minutes, look as far as you can for 60 seconds.

Mini Reset: Feel your mind stretch past the walls.

Whisper to Yourself: "I am allowed to expand."

---

3. Name What You Are Feeling

Naming softens chaos.

Story: When Leo learned to quietly name his feelings ("Anxious," "Tired," "Hopeful"), they lost their overwhelming edge. Emotions went from tidal waves to ripples he could ride.

Gentle Insight: Language turns turmoil into understanding.

Layer of Meaning: Naming is a form of self-rescue.

Try This Today: When overwhelmed, silently name what you feel without judgment.

Mini Reset: Breathe into the space that clarity creates.

Whisper to Yourself: "I can meet myself where I am."

---

4. The Five Senses Anchor

When your mind races, your body can ground you.

Tiny Practice:

- Name 5 things you can see.
  Name 4 things you can touch.
- Name 3 things you can hear.
- Name 2 things you can smell.
- Name 1 thing you can taste.

Story: During panic attacks, Zoe practiced the Five Senses Anchor. It pulled her back from fear into now.

Gentle Reflection: Your body is a loyal lighthouse.

Layer of Meaning: Presence is always waiting at your skin's edge.

Try This Today: Practice the Five Senses Anchor once today, even if you don't "need" it.

Mini Reset: Feel yourself come home.

Whisper to Yourself: "Now is safe enough."

Mini-Section - Stillness is Not Emptiness

Stillness can feel frightening if you're used to racing.

But stillness is not a void. It is a space where new breath, new thoughts, and new softness can enter.

Gentle Thought: Stillness doesn't erase you. It reveals you.

Gentle Practice: Sit quietly for one minute today. Watch what rises. Watch what softens.

Whisper to Yourself: "Stillness makes space for me."

Deep Story - The 3 - Minute Pause that Changed Everything

There was a day when everything felt wrong. Rushing emails, tense meetings, a sinking feeling inside my chest.

Instead of pushing harder, I did something unthinkable: I stopped.

I stepped outside. Set a timer for 3 minutes. And simply stood, feeling the breeze on my skin.

The world didn't fall apart. My tasks didn't vanish. But my mind, tight and frantic, softened. I returned to my desk breathing differently. Writing differently. Being different.

Gentle Thought: A moment of pause can redirect the whole river of your day.

Gentle Practice: Today, when you feel frantic, step away for 3 minutes. Just three.

Whisper to Yourself: "Three minutes can change everything.

Mini-Section - Permission to Pause

You do not need to earn your right to rest.

You do not need to wait until you are broken to stop and breathe.

Rest is not a reward. It is a rhythm.

Gentle Reflection: Pausing is not giving up. It is gathering strength.

Gentle Practice: Today, permit yourself to pause, without guilt, without needing to justify it.

Whisper to Yourself: "My being matters more than my doing."

Affirmations for Gentle Mental Reset

- "I am allowed to rest without apology."
- "One breath is enough to begin again."
- "I trust myself to slow down when needed."
- "My worth is not measured by my speed."
- "Stillness strengthens me."
- "I reset gently, I restart bravely."

Gentle Reminder: Speak to yourself the way you would to someone you deeply love.

Bonus Checklist - Tiny Mental Resets You Can Do Anytime

1-Minute Resets:

- One slow deep breath.
- Look out the window.
- Stretch your arms overhead.
- Name one feeling.
- Feel your feet on the ground.

5-Minute Resets:

- Step outside and feel the air.
- Write down 3 things you're grateful for.d
- Listen to a calming song.
- Close your eyes and scan your body.
- Doodle freely with no goal.

Gentle Reminder: Your mind deserves gentle tending.

BONUS PART 3 - Quotes for Gentle Living

1. "Small shifts birth great changes."

2. "You are allowed to start small and stay soft."

3. "Clearing space is claiming breath."

4. "Progress whispers, it rarely shouts."

5. "A tiny reset is still a reset."

6. "Stillness is a form of courage."

7. "Ease isn't laziness. It's wisdom dressed in softness."

8. "The home you create reflects the peace you cultivate."

9. "Begin with one square foot, one small kindness."

10. "Your worth is not measured by your productivity."

11. "Breath before bustle. Pause before panic."

12. "Release what no longer sings inside you."

13. "Tidy spaces invite restful hearts."

14. "You are not behind. You are becoming."

15. "Rest is not earned. Rest is essential."

16. "What you clear externally clears pathways internally."

17. "The gentler you move, the deeper you heal."

18. "Resets don't require a reason. Only permission."

19. "Mess is not failure. It's a snapshot of living."

20. "Your sanctuary grows with every tiny act of care."

21. "Perfection is brittle. Progress is supple."

22. "Start messy. Start scared. Just start."

23. "Your pace is enough."

24. "You are allowed to breathe, even here."

25. "Clarity loves simplicity."

26. "Every tiny reset is a vote for the life you want."

27. "You are not too late."

28. "Ease and effort can coexist."

29. "A calmer space nurtures a clearer mind."

30. "Progress made quietly is still progress."

31. "Systems aren't cages. They're bridges to ease."

32. "Stillness doesn't erase you. It reveals you."

33. "Release creates room for renewal."

34. "Messy beginnings lead to magnificent transformations."

35. "Honor your pauses. They are sacred ground."

36. "Decluttering is a love letter to your future self."

37. "Tiny victories count too."

38. "You deserve spaces that feel like exhaling."

39. "Even in chaos, you can carve out calm."

40. "Your life deserves a gentle rhythm, not a frantic race."

BONUS PART 4 - Worksheets & Exercises for Gentle Living

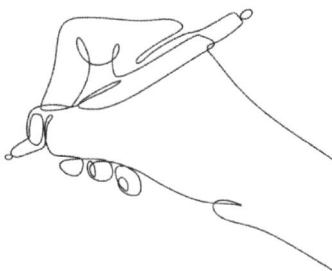

1. One-Square-Foot Rescue Map

Goal: Pick one tiny spot and fully reset it.

Instructions:

- Choose a small space (corner of a desk, part of a shelf).
- Sketch it or describe it briefly below.
- List what you need to remove or rearrange.
- Reset it with full presence.

My Space: _____

Things to Clear: _____

Things to Keep: _____

Date of Reset: _____

How I Felt After: _____

Gentle Whisper: "Even one tiny space can become a sanctuary."

---

2. Drop Zone Design Sheet

Goal: Create a "drop zone" for daily clutter.

Instructions:

- Choose where you need a drop zone (entryway, desk, kitchen counter).
- Decide what container or boundary you will use.

Location: _____

Container/Tool: _____

What Will Go There: _____

Gentle Whisper: "A thoughtful landing spot prevents scattered storms."

---

3. Emotional Energy Space Scan

Goal: Notice how spaces make you feel.

Instructions:

- Walk through your home slowly.
- In each area, note your gut feeling (calm, tense, overwhelmed, peaceful).

Living Room: _____

Bedroom: _____

Kitchen: _____

Workspace: _____

One Space I Want to Reset First: _____

Gentle Whisper: "Your body knows where peace is missing."

4. Gentle Weekly Reset Plan

Goal: Build a light rhythm of resets each week.

Instructions:

- Choose 3–5 small resets you will commit to weekly.

Example Resets:

- Clear kitchen counter.
- Reset the bedside table.
- Tidy bag or backpack.

My Gentle Reset Plan:

1. _____
2. _____
3. _____
4. _____
5. _____

Gentle Whisper: "Tiny threads of care weave strong safety nets."

5. Seasonal Refresh Checklist

Goal: Align your space with the seasons.

Instructions:

- Each new season, refresh 2–3 tiny areas.

Spring: _____

Summer: _____

Autumn: _____

Winter: _____

Gentle Whisper: "Every season asks different things of your heart and your home."

---

6. Digital Declutter Sprint

Goal: Clear digital clutter quickly.

Instructions:

- Set a timer for 20 minutes.

- Pick one digital area to declutter: Inbox, Photos, Downloads, or Apps.
- Celebrate every 10 items deleted.

Today's Focus: _____

Items Cleared: _____

Gentle Whisper: "Deleting is not losing. It is choosing clarity."

---

7. Tiny Mental Reset Tracker

Goal: Notice and nurture daily tiny resets.

Instructions:

- Each day, mark when you complete a tiny mental reset.
- It can be a deep breath, a stretch, naming an emotion, etc.

Day	Tiny Reset Completed? (Y/N)	How I Felt After
Mon		

Tue		
Wed		
Thu		
Fri		
Sat		
Sun		

Gentle Whisper: "Tiny steady acts build mighty calm."

CLOSING NOTE - BEGIN GENTLY, LIVE FULLY

If you take away only one thing from this book, let it be this:

You do not need to rush to transform your space, your habits, or your mind. Every small act - a single cleared corner, a quiet breath, a paused moment - plants a seed.

Your home is not a project to complete. Your life is not a checklist to finish. Your mind is not a machine to fix.

You are allowed to live in rhythms of gentleness. You are allowed to start messy. You are allowed to rest, to reset, to begin again as many times as you need.

Each tiny reset, each simple clearing, each quiet breath is a way of saying: "I am here. I am becoming."

May your days be lighter. May your spaces be softer. May your heart find steady ground, again and again.

Thank you for allowing this book to be a small part of your unfolding journey.

Gentle Whisper to Close: "You are already enough. You are already home."

ACKNOWLEDGMENTS

This book would not have been possible without the inspiration and support of so many beautiful souls.

First, a heartfelt thank you to you, the reader. Your courage to choose gentleness, your willingness to begin small, and your trust in tiny resets are what breathe life into these pages. If this book has brought even a little more lightness to your days, consider sharing it with someone you care about, because healing flows best when it is shared.

Special thanks to the Bring Hacks community for believing in the power of simple, actionable shifts. Your engagement, encouragement, and real-life transformations continue to inspire this work beyond measure.

Thank you for allowing this book to walk beside you for a little while.

CONTINUE YOUR JOURNEY

Your journey toward a lighter, gentler life doesn't have to end here.

Join the Community:
 Connect with like-minded souls who believe in tiny shifts and gentle living.
 Search "Life Hacks, Tips, Tricks" on Facebook.

Explore More:
 Discover daily hacks, inspirations, and gentle tools by downloading our app: **Bring Hacks**, available in your device's app store.

Unlock Bonus Hacks:
 Visit bringhacks.com to access exclusive hacks, tips, and resources designed to help you live lighter, breathe easier, and feel more at home - inside and out.

Tiny resets. Big peace.
 We'll meet you there.

A SMALL REQUEST

If this book brought a little more lightness, clarity, or gentleness into your days, would you consider leaving a review?

Your honest feedback helps other readers discover the book - and it helps tiny messages of hope travel even further.

You can leave a review where you purchased the book.

Thank you for being part of this journey.
 Every small act - even a review - creates ripples of kindness.

Printed in Dunstable, United Kingdom